61739
Dogteam

Gary Paulsen
AR B.L.: 3.2
Points: 0.5   LG

Dogteam

Dragonfly Books  New York

illustrated by Ruth Wright Paulsen

GARY PAULSEN

Dogteam

Published by Dragonfly Books
an imprint of
Random House Children's Books
a division of Random House, Inc.
1540 Broadway, New York, New York 10036

Visit us on the Web! www.randomhouse.com/kids

Educators and librarians, for a variety of teaching tools,
visit us at www.randomhouse.com/teachers

ISBN: 0-440-41130-0

Reprinted by arrangement with Delacorte Press

Printed in the United States of America

November 1995

10 9 8 7 6 5 4

Sometimes we run at night.

In the full moon when it is blue and
white on the snow at the same time,
so bright and clean and open
you could read in the dark,
we harness the dogs and run at night.

They tremble.

Some small songs of excitement when
the harnesses are put on because they want to run,
breathe to run, eat to run, live to run...

But silent. Straining to run, to go, to
join the snow and the moon and the night, pulling
against the tugs and the gangline tied to the
sled, heaving until, finally, the hook is freed
from the snow and they are gone.

The dance.

Through the trees, in and out, the sled whipping after them through the trees with no sound but the song of the runners, the high-soft-shusshh-whine of the runners and the soft jingle of their collars.

Into the night.

Away from camp, away from people, away from
houses and light and noise and into only the one thing,

into only winternight they fly away and away and away.

A lake.

Frozen and flat and white in the
moonlight we slip out of the woods
onto the ice and time for one breath,
two, and across, the ice gone,

creaking and moaning beneath us and into the
trees again, left, right, and we are not alone.

Wolves.

They come alongside in the moonlight,
moonwolves, snowwolves, nightwolves, they run with
us, pace the dogs, pace our hearts and our lives
and then turn, turn away in the blue dark.

And so we run.

Part of the night
and dark and cold

and moonlight and steam from our breaths,

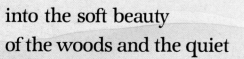

into the soft beauty
of the woods and the quiet

we run mile on mile until we see lights,

see lights and find that we have circled in the night,
circled in the snow and the winter and our lives
and all the world

and have come home.

There.

Gleaming yellow kitchen light, warm in
the cold, deep cold, cold so ice-breath freezes on
eyelids, freezes eyes shut; cold so the light from

the moon is frozen on the snow; cold so all the dogs are coated with ice and the snaps on their collars and harness won't open and their laughing-panting breath freezes on their cheeks and makes them all smiles, dogsmiles, doglaughs.

There.

Home.

And we stop. Close now, so close we see
people in the cabin, see the faces at the window.

The dogs look back.
Why are they still in harness?
Why are they standing?
The dance is over, is it not –
is not the dogdance
in the dogmoon
and dogcold
and dognight over?

Did you ... they sing, little jets of steam from their mouths.

Did you did you did you did you . . .
Did you want it to last forever?

About the Author and Illustrator

"Nothing in running dogs is quite so beautiful as a night run—the cold is crisper, the dogs run for the pure joy of running, and the moon seems to dance on the snow. In all of our running and training and raising puppies the night runs stand out the most," says Gary Paulsen.

Gary Paulsen is the author of many acclaimed books for young people, including three Newbery Honor books. He has twice run the Iditarod dogsled race across Alaska.

Ruth Wright Paulsen has been a working artist for twenty years and has illustrated many books, including Gary Paulsen's *The Haymeadow.* She also manages a seventy-dog kennel and helps train Iditarod dogs with her husband, Gary.

About the Book

The illustrations for this book were painted with Winsor & Newton watercolors on Lanaquarelle 140-pound cold press 100-percent rag watercolor paper. The text is set in 16-point Zapf International Light. Typography is by Lynn Braswell.